PENGUIN POETRY

DEFYING GRAVITY

Roger McGough was born in Liverpool and educated at St Mary's College and the University of Hull. He has been a writer for many years, and his numerous collections have established him as one of the most distinctive and powerful voices in contemporary poetry. His books include *Watchwords*, *After the Merrymaking*, *Gig*, *Sporting Relations*, *In the Glassroom*, *Unlucky for Some*, *Holiday on Death Row*, *Waving at Trains*, *Melting into the Foreground* (Penguin 1987), *Summer with Monika* (revised Penguin 1990) and *Selected Poems 1967–1987*, *Vol. 1 Blazing Fruit* (Penguin 1990) and *Vol. 2 You at the Back*; and, for children, *The Great Smile Robbery*, *Sky in the Pie*, *Noah's Ark*, *The Stowaways*, *Nailing the Shadow*, *An Imaginary Menagerie*, *Helen Highwater*, *Counting by Numbers*, *The Lighthouse that Ran Away*, *Pillow Talk* and *Lucky*. Roger McGough now lives in London.

ROGER McGOUGH

DEFYING GRAVITY

PENGUIN BOOKS

The poem 'Defying Gravity'
is for John Hewson

PENGUIN BOOKS

Published by the Penguin Group
Penguin Books Ltd, 27 Wrights Lane, London W8 5TZ, England
Penguin Books USA Inc., 375 Hudson Street, New York, New York 10014, USA
Penguin Books Australia Ltd, Ringwood, Victoria, Australia
Penguin Books Canada Ltd, 10 Alcorn Avenue, Toronto, Ontario, Canada M4V 3B2
Penguin Books (NZ) Ltd, 182–190 Wairau Road, Auckland 10, New Zealand

Penguin Books Ltd, Registered Offices: Harmondsworth, Middlesex, England

First published by Viking 1992
Published in Penguin Books 1993
1 3 5 7 9 10 8 6 4 2

The Elements sequence was first published in the
Channel 4 book *An A–Z of the Elements*,
which accompanied the film *Equinox: The Elements*,
produced by Windfall Films for Channel 4 in 1991

The lines quoted as an epigraph to 'The Darling Buds of Maybe' are from
'This be The Verse' by Philip Larkin, published in the collection *High Windows*
by Faber and Faber Ltd. Reproduced by permission of the publishers

Printed in England by Clays Ltd, St Ives plc

Contents

1

The Railings 5

Squaring Up 6

Snowing Down South 7

Spitting Prohibited 8

How to Become a Sixer 10

Maurice 11

Alphabet Soup 12

Wearing Thin 14

Sacrifices 15

Having My Ears Boxed 16

Hard Times 18

Bath – Avon 20

2

The Darling Buds of Maybe 23

This be Another Verse 24

Big Ifs 25

The Poet Takes an Autumnal Stroll on Hampstead Heath 26

Creative Writing 26

A Critic Reviews the Curate's Egg 27

The Nearest Forty-two 27

Word Trap 28

Planet Babel 29

Children's Writer 30

Joinedupwriting 31

It's Only a P . . . 32
It's Only a P . . . Part Two 33
Awful Acrobats 34

3
The City of London Tour 39
Five-car Family 40
Stinging in the Rain 42
Curse 43
Repelled by Metal 44
Neighbourhood Watch 45
Poem against Capital Punishment 45
Fired with Enthusiasm 46
Shavings Account 46
Another Mid-life Crisis 47
Early Morning Poems 48
Rocker-by 49
Used to Drink 50
Where It's At 52
Fart 54
No Surprises 56

4
Crazy Bastard 59
Your Favourite Hat 60
As Every Bandage Dreams 62
Fear of Flares 63
The Fly 64
Behemoth 65
Ex Patria 65

Isolation 66
Two Quatrains 67
The Blues 68
Star Juice 69
The Bright Side 70
The Unknown Worrier 71
Five Ways to Help You Pass Safely through a Dark Wood Late at Night 72

5
Poor Old Dead Horses 75
The Trouble with Snowmen 76
Getting On 78
Getting Off 78
Just Passing 79
In at the Kill 80
Cinders 82
Who are These Men? 84
Four Sons 85
Bearhugs 86
Defying Gravity 88
The Man in the Moon 90

6 The Elements
Oxygen 93
Nitrogen 94
Carbon 96
Iron 98
Mercury 100
Sulphur 102

Gold 104
Fool's Gold 106
Element 109 107

Defying Gravity

1

The Railings

You came to watch me playing cricket once.
Quite a few of the fathers did.
At ease, outside the pavilion
they would while away a Saturday afternoon.
Joke with the masters, urge on
their flannelled offspring. But not you.

Fielding deep near the boundary
I saw you through the railings.
You were embarrassed when I waved
and moved out of sight down the road.
When it was my turn to bowl though
I knew you'd still be watching.

Third ball, a wicket, and three more followed.
When we came in at the end of the innings
the other dads applauded and joined us for tea.
Of course, you had gone by then. Later,
you said you'd found yourself there by accident.
Just passing. Spotted me through the railings.

* * *

Speech-days · Prize-givings · School-plays
The Twentyfirst · The Wedding · The Christening
You would find yourself there by accident.
Just passing. Spotted me through the railings.

Squaring Up

When I was thirteen and crimping my first quiff
Dad bought me a pair of boxing-gloves
In the hope that I would aspire to the Noble Art.

But I knew my limitations from the start:
Myopia, cowardice and the will to come second.
But I feigned enthusiasm for his sake.

Straight after tea, every night for a week
We would go a few rounds in the yard.
Sleeves rolled-up, collarless and gloveless

He would bob and weave and leave me helpless.
Uppercuts would tap me on the chin
Left hooks muss my hair, haymakers tickle my ear.

Without glasses, only one thing was clear:
The fact that I was hopeless. He had a son
Who couldn't square up. So we came to blows.

Losing patience, he caught me on the nose.
I bled obligingly. A sop. A sacrifice.
Mum threw in the towel and I quit the ring.

But when the bell goes each birthday I still feel the sting
Not of pain, but of regret. You said sorry
And you were. I didn't. And I wasn't.

Snowing Down South

'It's snowing down south,' one girl would say
When another's petticoat showed beneath the skirt
And, giggling, they would rush off to the Ladies.

Modesty restored, they would return to the floor
And dance demurely, with a poise we could not match
We boys, who stood pretending not to watch.

Then half an hour or so before the Last Waltz
The DJ would put on some rock 'n' roll
And emboldened with ale, we'd form a ring.

Eyes closed, they'd spin, those girls, skirts swirling high
To reveal . . . Need I go on? Mid-fifties.
You've seen the pictures, heard the songs.

In the spotlight of our lascivious gaze
Fired by the rhythm, our whistles and screeches
Down south, suddenly, everything is peaches.

Spitting Prohibited

When I was a boy (cue Brass Band)
A notice downstairs on every bus and tram
Said: NO SMOKING. SPITTING PROHIBITED.

Then overnight, or so it seemed, things changed.
The second part was painted over
And the sign said simply: NO SMOKING.

Imagine that first morning, when passengers,
Bleary-eyed, looked up and saw,
By omission, an invitation.

Then did everybody, unrestrained,
Leap up, clear their throats and let rip?
Expectorate to their lungs' content?

Did drip, dribble, spurt and spatter?
Hawk and croak until the windows were steaming
And the passageways awash?

Transport Committee met and unanimously agreed
That every by-law be clearly stated
And the notice then to read:

NO SMOKING. SPITTING PROHIBITED.
PLEASE REFRAIN FROM URINATING AND DEFECATING,
SOLICITING AND IMPORTUNING.

FORNICATION AND BESTIALITY FORBIDDEN.
ARSON, RAPE AND PILLAGE NOT PERMITTED.
(STRICTLY, NO BRASS BANDS.)

How to Become a Sixer

Wait until Akela is out of the room
and the noise level begins to rise.
As soon as you hear returning footsteps
call out in a loud, clear voice:
'Quiet everybody. We promised to get on
with things in silence. DYB. DYB. DYB. Remember?'

By now the footsteps will have stopped
and the Pack looking to see if you are being serious.
Ignore them, and use the pause
to do something useful, like tying a knot.
Akela will then make stamping noises
and open the door. Everything is shipshape.

Acknowledge the appraising glance
but appear embarrassed, as if you wished
you could bite your tongue off.
Promotion will quickly follow. And disappointment:
Akela in a tent, unfurling his knob.
Dirty Old Bugger. DOB. DOB. DOB.

Maurice

There were no 'gays' in those days, only 'funny' men.
Enter Mrs Thomas: 'He's a bit effeminate
That Maurice. "Funny", if you ask me.

Bringing his "friend" home on leave
The two of them in bed and her bringing in the tea.
His own mother not knowing. It will end in tears.

What do they call themselves nowadays?
Course, she brought it all on herself. (Queers!
That's it.) Spoiled from the word go.

Too nesh to play out in the street.
The other boys were rough, and Ho! Ho!
He might be led astray. Him, led astray?

Mind you, it's none of my business
Live and let live, that's what I say.
Although, to be honest, if I had my way

I'd put the pair of them on show in the zoo.
I mean, what do they see in each other?
I mean, what do they actually, pardon the expression, do?'

Alphabet Soup

Whenever I went into our local library
I would take out a book for my dad.
An adventure yarn. Something to do with the sea.

Occasionally, I'd bring home one he'd read before.
'Doesn't matter,' he would say, 'it's a good 'un.'
And settling down, sign on for the same voyage.

It wasn't laziness on his part, but a kind of fear.
Libraries were for educated people.
Full of traps. Procedures. Forms to fill in.

They would notice his handwriting wasn't joined up
So then they would try and catch him out.
Ask questions about Shakespeare. About proper books.

* * *

Although a stevedore (Mum preferred that to 'docker')
And landlubbered all his married life
He'd have passed four-square on seamanship.

Because he'd been to sea himself when young
And would often talk, with some regret,
Of how he'd nearly jumped ship in Fremantle.

He loved the solitude of the bush. Its stillness,
And the sky a blueprint for eternity.
'And the names of the places. Now that's poetry!'

I picture ourselves in the outback
The nearest library five hundred miles away
Him, married to a girl from Manjimup
Me, trying to make sense of alphabet soup.

Wearing Thin

'You'll soon grow into it,' she would say
When buying a school blazer three sizes too big.
And she was right as mothers usually are.

Syrup of figs. Virol. Cod liver oil.
Within a year I did grow into it
By then, of course, it was threadbare.

Pulling in different directions
My clothes and I never matched.
And in changing-rooms nothing has changed.

I can buy what I like and when
New clothes that are a perfect fit.
Full-length mirror, nervous grin,
It's me now that's threadbare, wearing thin.

Sacrifices

I was forever hearing about the sacrifices
My parents made.
Little ones almost daily
Big ones when required.

Having me meant sacrifices. Going without.
And then to cap it all, the Scholarship:
School uniforms, violin lessons,
Elocution, extra tuition.

'If it's not one thing it's another.
I hope you're worth it.' But was I?
The dictionary confirmed my doubts:
'*Sacrifice*, a ritual killing of a person
or animal with the intention of pleasing a deity.'

Sacrifice. No, I wasn't worth it.
All that blood for a few O-levels.

Having My Ears Boxed

I am waiting in the corridor
To have my ears boxed.
I am nervous, for Mr O'Hanlon
Is a beast of his word.

For the last twenty minutes
I have let my imagination
Run away with itself.
But I am too scared to follow.

Will he use that Swiss Army knife
To slice through cleanly? Bite them off?
Tear carefully along perforated lines?
Tug sharply like loose Elastoplasts?

Acknowledging the crowd's roar
Will he hold my head aloft
As if it were the FA Cup
And pull the handles? Aagghhrr . . .

And then the box. Cardboard?
Old cigar-box possibly? Or a pair?
Separate coffins of polished pine.
L and R. 'Gone to a better place.'

Impatient now, I want to get it
Over with. Roll on four o'clock.
When, hands over where-my-ears-used-to-be
I run the gauntlet of jeering kids.

At six, mother arrives home weary
After a hard day at the breadcrumb factory.
I give her the box. She opens it
And screams something. I say:

'Pardon?'

Hard Times

(i)

Each year, in early December
Grandma would oblige
by falling over
and dislocating something

In hospital, on Christmas Day
all the family would visit
Sit round the bed
and gobble up her dinner.

(ii)

To eke out extra money
during the summer holidays
my schoolfriends and I
would go nit-picking

Conditions were terrible
and the pay was poor
But there were perks:
We were allowed to keep the eggs.

(iii)

If we could have afforded a bath
We would have had the best. A fine one.
Iron. Broad as a bed, deep as the ocean.
Standing on wingèd feet, proud as a lion.

And oh, what coal we would have stored in it.
Nuggets, big as babies' heads, still blinking
In the daylight. Black as wedding-boots,
So polished you could see your face in them.

And oh, what stories we might have told.
Seated round the hearth on winter nights
The fire crackling, the flames leaping.
Amber liquor sparkling in crystal glasses.

Unfortunately, we were too poor to know stories.

Bath – Avon

I have a problem with Bath.
I use the short *a*, rhyming it with *math*,
Whereas southerners put in the *r*. *Barth*.

So my living there would be a kind of hell
(Although a lovely place by all accounts).
Never have an operation you cannot spell
Or live in a town you mispronounce.

2

Get out as early as you can,
And don't have any kids yourself.

'Perfick,' said Old Larkin
The last kid put to bed
He took the Missus in his arms
Gave her a kiss and said:

'I'll pop out for a quick one
If that's all right with you?
I'll not be long, I promise
'Cos I've got work to do.'

'You mean the roof,' said Ma,
'You're going to mend that leak.'
Philip stopped.
'No, "This Be The Verse",'
That final stanza's too bleak.'

This be Another Verse

They don't fuck you up, your mum and dad
(Despite what Larkin says)
It's other grown-ups, other kids
Who, in their various ways

Die. And their dying casts a shadow
Numbering all our days
And we try to keep from going mad
In multifarious ways.

And most of us succeed, thank God,
So if, to coin a phrase
You're fucked up, don't blame your mum and dad
(Despite what Larkin says).

Big Ifs

To the mourners round his deathbed
William Blake was moved to say:
'Oh, if only I had taken
The time to write that play.'

Nor was William Shakespeare
Finally satisfied:
'I know there's a novel in me.'
(No sooner said than died.)

Beethoven in his darkest hour
Over and over he railed:
'If only I had learned guitar
Before my hearing failed.'

In the transept of St Paul's
Slumped Sir Christopher Wren:
'I'd give them something really good
If I could only do it again.'

Leonardo, Mozart, Rembrandt
Led sobbing through the Pearly Gates:
'If only I'd have . . .
I could have been one of the Greats.'

The Poet Takes an Autumnal Stroll on Hampstead Heath

Light rain, like steam
from a cup of camomile tea
poured from a copper kettle
heated o'er a sandalwood fire
bids him return home
and consider an alternative career.

Creative Writing

Why can't I teach Creative Writing in Minnesota?
Or, better still, be Poet in Residence at Santa Fe?
Where golden-limbed girls with a full quota
Of perfect teeth lionize me, feed me, lead me astray.

A professorship, perhaps, visiting in Ann Arbor?
(Nothing too strenuous, the occasional social call.)
What postcards I can write, what ambitions I can harbour:
Hawaii in the springtime, Harvard in the fall.

A Critic Reviews the Curate's Egg

'It's all bad.
Especially in parts.'

The Nearest Forty-two

I want to write a new poem.
What words shall I choose?
I go in. The variety is endless.
Images stretch into infinity.

I dither. Can't make up my mind.
Inspiration becomes impatient.
Stamps its feet. Panicking
I grab the nearest forty-two,

Word Trap

Sometimes they trap me
Stop me in my tracks.

Thinking my way through
Towards a promising idea

When I am distracted
By a sound. A spelling crackles.

Without a second thought
I am off into the thicket.

The next thing I know
It is time for bed.

Another poem finished
And nothing said.

Planet Babel

'I found I could not use the long line because of my nervous nature.'

– William Carlos Williams

As soon as my voice is heard above the babble
Which ceases as people turn
I want to disappear. Hide under the table.

My pulse races and I consequently gabble.
Puzzled faces make mine burn
And make it crystal clear – I'm from Planet Babel.

Children's Writer

John in the garden
Playing goodies and baddies

Janet in the bedroom
Playing mummies and daddies

Mummy in the kitchen
Washing and wiping

Daddy in the study
Stereotyping

Joinedupwriting

From the first
tentative scratch on the wall
To the final
unfinished, hurried scrawl:
One poem.

It's Only a P . . .

Feeling a trifle smug after breaking off an untidy,
Drawn-out affair with somebody I no longer fancied
I was strolling through Kensington Gardens
When who should I bump into but Gavin.

Gavin, I should point out, is the husband.
'I'm worried about Lucy,' he said, straight out.
'I don't blame you,' I thought, but said nothing.
'Suspect she's having an affair. Any ideas?'

'Divorce,' I suggested. 'You might even get custody.'
'No, I mean Lucy,' he persisted. 'Who with?'
We walked on in silence, until casually, I asked:
'An affair, you say, what makes you so convinced?'

He stopped and produced from an inside pocket
A sheet of paper which I recognized at once.
It was this poem. Handwritten, an early draft.
Then I saw the gun. 'For God's sake, Gavin,
It's only a p . . .

It's Only a P . . . Part Two

A shot rang out. The bullet was not intended for me.
It embedded itself harmlessly into a tall sycamore.
(Harmlessly, that is, except for the tall sycamore.)
Gavin pocketed the gun. I was shaking like a leaf.

I seized his arm. 'It's over now,' I stammered
'There was nothing in it really. A moment of madness.'
I was lying and wondered if he could tell.
He gave no sign, so relaxing my grip we walked on.

'You'd better have this,' he said, and held out the poem.
'But I'd rather you didn't publish. Spare my blushes.'
I took it. 'If not for me for Lucy's sake.'
'Trust me,' I said and crumpled it into a ball.

Behind us, the sycamore rose swaying from the bushes,
Staggered across the ornamental lake
And collapsed against a wall.

Awful Acrobats

Poets make awful acrobats.
Good at barely moving
Idle musing has impaired
Their sense of balance.

Once the horizon tilts
Everything begins to slide:
Cups and saucers, trees,
Buildings, spirit-levels.

Out of touch with the ground
They are out of touch with themselves.
Struggling to make sense of air
They become entangled with it.

The roll of drums:
A few floppy cartwheels
A crumpled somersault
Then up on to the high wire . . .

After the first falter, the fall.
It is faultless. The safety-net
Holds out its arms. The poet

misses.

(Gravity hangs its head in shame.)

* * *

Poets have a way with language
A certain jauntiness with hats

They can make a decent curry
And are very fond of cats

Though some are closet fascists
In the main they're democrats

But all things being considered
Poets make awful acrobats.

3

The City of London Tour

'Along Leadladen Street
Into Snarl-up Close
Through Crosspatch
Into Coronary Circus

Past Foulmouth Gardens
Into Fetid Lane
Along Profligate
To the station at Charnel House

Up Dirtneedle Street
Into Destitute Square
Down Pacemaker Passage
(Nearly there)

A quick one in the "Half Lung"
(Leave your gasmask at the door)
Which concludes, ladies and gents,
The City of London Tour.'

Five-car Family

We're a five-car family
We got what it takes
Eight thousand cc
Four different makes

One each for the kids
I run two
One for the missus
When there's shopping to do

Cars are Japanese of course
Subaru and Mazda
And the Nissan that the missus takes
Nippin down to Asda

We're a load of noisy parkers
We never do it neat
Drive the neighbours crazy
When we take up half the street

Unleaded petrol?
That's gotta be a joke
Stepping on the gas we like
The smoke to make you choke

Carbon monoxide
Take a deep breath
Benzine dioxide
Automanic death

'Cos it's all about noise
And it's all about speed
And it's all about power
And it's all about greed

And it's all about fantasy
And it's all about dash
And it's all about machismo
And it's all about cash

And it's all about blood
And it's all about gore
And it's all about oil
And it's all about war

And it's all about money
And it's all about spend
And it's all about time
That it came to an end.

Stinging in the Rain

Stinging in the rain   I'm
Stinging in the rain   My
Skin is peeling   I'm
Stinging in the rain   I

Don't like the feeling   I
Can't stand the pain   It's
Burning my flesh   And
Boiling my brain   The

Buildings are melting   I
Can't take the strain   There's
Blood on the sidewalk   I'm
Going insane   I'm

Crying and frying   And
Dying in vain   I'm
Stinging just stinging
In the stinking acid
(What a glorious feeling) . . .

Curse

Cyanide in the forest
Dead fish in the sea
A loaded gun
Where the sun should be

May those who sold us
Down the river
As polluted
As the lies they told

Find their banknotes
Carcinogenic
Nuclear active
Their gold.

Repelled by Metal

I don't drive, I'm afraid.
Never had the inclination or the need.
Being antimagnetic, I am repelled by metal
And unimpressed by speed.

Nor am I being 'holier than thou'.
Thou art a godsend to be candid
You with the car and the welcoming smile
Without your lift I'd be stranded.

And it's not that I dislike cars
Though noisy and dangerous I dare say
Money-eaters and poison-excreters, okay
But I don't dislike cars, per se.

It's just that I know my limitations.
I'd be all thumbs behind a wheel.
Don't laugh. Could you park a poem
In a space this small? Well, that's how I feel.

Neighbourhood Watch

It's a sin
It's a crime
Now we can't tell the time
Our neighbourhood watch
Has been stolen!

Poem against Capital Punishment

I live in the Capital
and it's punishment.

Fired with Enthusiasm

This morning
the boss
came into work
bursting
with enthusiasm

and fired everybody

Shavings Account

'Not to put too fine a point on it,'
Said the Bank Manager, pushing my finger
Into the desk-top pencil-sharpener,
'But you have a larger overdraft
Than I had given you credit for.'

He turned the handle. Turned the screw.
'Sorry, there's nothing we can do.
Business is business, we need our pound of flesh.
Next finger please. Put it in and . . . PUSH . . .'

Another Mid-life Crisis

3 a.m. Feeling like death
and wanting to end it all
I reach for the aspirin bottle.
Will there be enough?

One by one I count them out. 72?
Need more to be on the safe side.
Rummaging around I add another 30.
That should do it.

Take the first two with a glass of water.
Feel better. Go back to bed. Fall asleep.

Early Morning Poems

(i)

Got up
did my toilet:
Washed
Shaved
Combed hair

My toilet looks much nicer now.

(ii)

Got up
Had shave
Did *Times* crossword

Had another shave.

Rocker-by

Hush-a-bye, Daddy, don't you cry
Baby will sing a lullaby

Your duck's arse
is thinning and grey
Your Elvis tattoo
is wearing away

Your bootlace ties
hang limp and frayed
Your 78s
are overplayed

Not rock 'n' roll
but aches 'n' pains
Drainies play hell
with varicose veins

Your blue-suede shoes
now have lead in them
Drunk each night
you go to bed in them
When the music stops
You'll be dead in them

Shush, old man, your day is done
Where mine has only just begun

Used to Drink

Used to drink Pernod
Till my insides, an inferno
Said 'No'

Schooners of sherry
Soon as merry
Sick, very

So I drank rum
Yo ho ho as they come
Sore bum

What's nice is
Gin with lemon slices
Made me grin. Did me in

Turned to lager (Special Brew)
Went gaga
So will you

Downed tequila
Soon down at heel, ah
It's a killer

Odd dram of malt
Gave the old liver a jolt
Called a halt.

Mineral water
Herb tea
Beers (alcohol-free)
Cheers! I deserve a pat on the back . . .

(Next year maybe give up cocaine and smack.)

Where It's At

I'm in the Health Club
I'm where it's at
Twenty minutes on the mat
Light circuit-training
Gentle jog if not raining
Sauna, jacuzzi
Sit by Suzi

I'm in the Wine Bar
I'm where it's at
Vino tinto into that
Pig out on tapas
Choose momento, make a pass
Scusi scusi
Chat up Suzi

I'm in the Porsche
I'm where it's at
Rocks off in Docklands' flat
Ecstasy, share a smoke
His 'n' hers, two lines of coke
CD something bluesy
Hold tight Suzi

I'm in prison
I'm where it's at
Didn't see the Passat. Splat!
Banged up on Isle of Wight
With terrorist and transvestite
Can't be choosy
Bye bye Suzi.

Fart

He was lyin there, so I . . . er
Stabbed him. Just the once.
In the stomach. Crashed out
on the sofa he was. After the pub.

He wasn't asleep. Some nights
he'd pass out but most nights he'd pretend.
Lie there he would, eyes closed.
Burp. Fart, like I wasn't there.

Eggin me on to say somethin.
And if I did. If ever I did,
you know, say what I thought
He'd be up in a flash.

Because that's what he wanted
Me to say somethin. Lose my temper.
I'd goaded him, you see. Asked for it.
'You asked for it,' he'd say

Afterwards, in bed, me, sobbin.
A fresh bruise on an old swellin.
Not on the face. He never hit me
on the face. Too calculatin.

Always the body. Stomach, kidneys
He used to be one of you, see.
He knew where to hit.
Cold. Always, in control.

But tonight, I took control.
Picked up the breadknife.
He was gettin ready to let one go
I could see that.

The veins in his neck standin out
Throbbin. White against the purple.
Eyes behind closed lids, flickerin
Waitin to jump out on me.

So I . . . er stabbed him. Just the once.
He farted and screamed at the same time.
I know that sounds funny, but it wasn't
Not at the time. Not with the blood.

He rolled off of the sofa
Hunched on his knees, holdin the knife.
Not tryin to pull it out
Just holdin it. Like keepin it in.

Then he keeled over and that was that.
I put my coat on and came down here
And what I want to know is . . .
What's goin to happen to the kids?

No Surprises

He wakes when the sun rises
Gets up   Exercises
Breakfasts with one whom he despises
Chooses one of his disguises
and his gun   Fires his
first bullet   It paralyses
Drives into town   Terrorizes
Armed police in visors
materialize   His demise is
swift   No surprises.

4

Crazy Bastard

I have always enjoyed the company of extroverts.
Wild-eyed men who would go too far
Up to the edge, and beyond. Mad, bad women.

Overcautious, me. Sensible shoes and a scarf
Tucked in. I never courted Danger
For fear of being rebuffed: 'Piss off, Four Eyes.'

*   *   *

Midsummer's eve in the sixties.
On a moonlit beach in Devon we sit around a fire
Drinking wine and cider. Someone strumming a guitar.

Suddenly, a girl strips off and runs into the sea.
Everybody follows suit, a whoop of flickering nakedness
Hot gold into cold silver.   Far out.

Not wanting to be last in I unbutton my jeans.
Then pause. Someone had better stay behind
And keep an eye on the clothes. Common sense.

I throw another piece of driftwood on to the fire
Above the crackle listen to the screams and the laughter
Take a long untroubled swig of scrumpy. Crazy bastard.

Your Favourite Hat

Believe me when I tell you that
I long to be your favourite hat

The velvet one. Purply-black
With ribbons trailing at the back

The one you wear to parties, plays,
Assignations on red-letter days

Like a bat in your unlit hall
I'd hang until there came the call

To freedom. To hug your crown
As you set off through Camden Town

To run my fingers through your hair
Unbeknown in Chalcot Square

To let them linger, let them trace
My shadow cast upon your face

Until, on reaching the appointed place
(The pulse at your temple, feel it race!)

Breathless, you whisper: 'At last, at last.'
And once inside, aside I'm cast

There to remain as time ticks by
Nap rising at each moan and sigh

Ecstatic, curling at the brim
To watch you naked, there with him

Until, too soon, the afternoon gone
You retrieve me, push me on

Then take your leave (as ever, in haste)
Me eager to devour the taste

Of your hair. Your temples now on fire
My tongue, the hatband as you perspire

To savour the dampness of your skin
As you window-gaze. Looking in

But not seeing. Over Primrose Hill
You dawdle, relaxed now, until

Home Sweet Home, where, safely back
Sighing, you impale me on the rack

Is it in spite or because of that
I long to be your favourite hat?

As Every Bandage Dreams

As every bandage dreams
of being the Shroud of Turin
So do I dream
of enfolding you

As every aria longs
for Pavarotti's velvet tongue
So my body yearns
to interpret you

As every avalanche schemes
the ascent of Everest
So I aspire
to the view from your summit

As every oilslick licks its lips
at the thought of the Galapagos
So I long to stick around
and pound your beaches

As everything that is without feeling
Comes to life when put next to you
So do I.

Fear of Flares

I have this fear:
At a glittering occasion,
some kind of ceremony,
I am waiting in line
to be introduced to Princess Di
when I realize that I am wearing
flared trousers. Flared trousers!

There is no time to lose.
Unzipping them, I let them fall
around my ankles, then stand back
to attention. Her Royal Highness,
to her credit, makes no mention,
chats amiably, then moves on.
I pull them up. No harm done.

The Fly

I'm sorry, God, I cannot love
The fly
No matter how I try.

Floaters, bloated on dead flesh
And faeces
Lovers of the stale and the excreted
A species
I wish could be deleted.

I'm sorry, God, but why oh why
Did you create
The common fly?

Spiders I can abide when they approach
At a push, not crush a scuttling roach
But the fly I hate to bits.
Brings out in me a deathwish.
Its.

I'm sorry, God, I cannot lie
This morning I   a fly.
And it felt good.

Behemoth

Be he moth
or be he not
He be noth
ing when I swat

Ex Patria

After supper, we move out on to the veranda.
Moths flit between lamps. We drink, think about sex
and consider how best to wreck each other's lives.

At the river's edge, the kitchen maids are washing up.
In the age-old tradition, they slap the plates
against the side of a rock, singing tonelessly.

Like tiny chauffeurs, the mosquitoes will soon arrive
and drive us home. O England, how I miss you.
Ascot, Henley, Wimbledon. It's the little things.

Isolation

I like my isolation
Within easy reach of other people's
Wide-open spaces set me on edge
Than a bland Savannah I'd rather be
Something clumped beneath a hedge

The Surrealist Stripper

I made you look
I made you stir
Do you like
My cubic hair?

The Capitalist Model

'You'd like a more
Seductive posture?
That's what I'm for
But it'll cost yer.'

The Blues

Two a.m.
in the Blue Magnolia.
I smoke my last cigarette
and wait for the piano-player
to send me a drink over.

Star Juice

This morning
came a loud moaning
as a cloud
clutching its stomach
staggered across the sky
and threw up
all over Manchester

I know the feeling
It's been up all night
drinking with the moon
Star juice
It's a killer.

The Bright Side

Things are so bad
I am reduced to scraping
The outside of the barrel.

And yet, I do not despair.
In the yard there are many
Worse off than myself. (Well, four:

A one-eyed rat
A three-legged cat
A corpse and the lavatory door.)

The Unknown Worrier

Don't worry, I'll do it for you
I'm a therapist *manqué*
Let me be your worry beads
I'll tell your cares away

Should I chance to sit beside you
In a café or a park
And a cloud is hanging over
Groaning, heavy and dark

You can bet that when it's time to go
You'll have nothing on your mind
While I sit in the shadow
Of the cloud you left behind

Don't worry, I'll do it for you
Relax, I'll take the strain
Anxiety is my forte
I've got worry on the brain

Five Ways to Help You Pass Safely through a Dark Wood Late at Night

1. Whistle a tune your father whistled
 when you were a child

2. Cross the first two fingers
 of your left hand

3. If you lose sight of the moon
 hold it in the mind's eye

4. Imagine the colours that surround you
 waiting for the first kiss of morning

5. Keep a Smith & Wesson in the glove
 compartment

5

Poor Old Dead Horses

Don't give your rocking-horse
To the old rag and bony

He'll go straight to the knacker
And haggle for money

The stirrups are torn off
The bridle and harness

Chopped up for firewood
It is thrown on the furnace

And the water that boils
Is chucked down the sluices

To wash away what remains
Of poor old dead horses.

The Trouble with Snowmen

'The trouble with snowmen,'
Said my father one year
'They are no sooner made
Than they just disappear.

I'll build you a snowman
And I'll build it to last
Add sand and cement
And then have it cast.

And so every winter,'
He went on to explain
'You shall have a snowman
Be it sunshine or rain.'

* * *

And that snowman still stands
Though my father is gone
Out there in the garden
Like an unmarked gravestone.

Staring up at the house
Gross and misshapen
As if waiting for something
Bad to happen.

For as the years pass
And I grow older
When summers seem short
And winters colder.

The snowmen I envy
As I watch children play
Are the ones that are made
And then fade away.

Getting On

The husk may crack
The chalksticks creak
The brain confused
The pulse is weak

But Time is your own, at least
And that beast, Passion
No longer screams to be fed.

Getting Off

I closed my eyes, held my breath
and tried to lie quite still
Refused to believe that death
applied to me, until

Just Passing

Just passing, I spot you through the railings.
You don't see me. Why should you?
Outside the gates, I am out of your orbit.

Break-time for Infants and first-year Juniors
and the playground is a microcosmos:
planets, asteroids, molecules, chromosomes.

Constellations swirling, a genetic whirlpool
Worlds within worlds. A Russian doll
of universes bursting at each seam.

Here and there, some semblance of order
as those who would benefit from rules
are already seeking to impose them.

Not yet having to make sense of it all
you are in tune with chaos, at its centre.
Third son lucky, at play, oblivious of railings.

I try and catch your eye. To no avail.
Wave goodbye anyway, and pocketing
my notebook, move on. Someday we must talk.

In at the Kill

The contractions are coming faster now.
Every ten minutes or so
A crush of pain made bearable
Only by the certainty of its passing.

Midwives come and go.
At nine forty-five, a show.
It must go on. The floodgates open,
A universe implodes.

There is no going back now
(As if there ever was). Shall I slip away
And start a new life?
Instead, I do as I am told:

'Push, push. Stop, stop. Now push.
Come on, more. The head's coming.
Push harder. Harder. Push, push.'
Then out it comes – whoosh.

Uncoiled, I am thrown back.
For some reason I twirl.
Doubledizzy, I steady myself
On the bedrail. 'It's a girl.'

* * *

And so it is. My first.
Having witnessed three sons bawl into view
With the familiar appendage of their gender,
I am unprepared for . . . (what's the word,

Begins with *p* and ends with *enda*?)
Amazed, not by any lack or absence
But by the prominence of the lack,
The perfect shape of the absence.

Flashbulbs interrupt my musing,
The theatre fills with flowers.
My wife leads the applause,
I bow. 'Thank you . . . Thank you . . .'

Cinders

After the pantomime, carrying you back to the car
On the coldest night of the year
My coat, black leather, cracking in the wind.

Through the darkness we are guided by a star
It is the one the Good Fairy gave you
You clutch it tightly, your magic wand.

And I clutch you tightly for fear you blow away
For fear you grow up too soon and – suddenly,
I almost slip, so take it steady down the hill.

Hunched against the wind and hobbling
I could be mistaken for your grandfather
And sensing this, I hold you tighter still.

Knowing that I will never see you dressed for the Ball
Be on hand to warn you against Prince Charmings
And the happy ever afters of pantomime.

On reaching the car I put you into the baby seat
And fumble with straps I have yet to master
Thinking, if only there were more time. More time.

You are crying now. Where is your wand?
Oh no. I can't face going back for it
Let some kid find it in tomorrow's snow.

Waiting in the wings, the witching hour.
Already the car is changing. Smells sweet
Of ripening seed. We must go. Must go.

Who are These Men?

Who are these men who would do you harm?
Not the mad-eyed who grumble at pavements
Banged up in a cell with childhood ghosts

Who shout suddenly and frighten you. Not they.
The men who would do you harm have gentle voices
Have practised their smiles in front of mirrors.

Disturbed as children, they are disturbed by them.
Obsessed. They wear kindness like a carapace
Day-dreaming up ways of cajoling you into the car.

Unattended, they are devices impatient
To explode. Ignore the helping hand
It will clench. Beware the lap, it is a trapdoor.

They are the spies in our midst. In the park,
Outside the playground, they watch and wait.
Given half a chance, love, they would take you

Undo you. Break you into a million pieces.
Perhaps, in time, I would learn forgiveness.
Perhaps, in time, I would kill one.

Four Sons (*A Wish*)

One son at each corner
of the bed
on which I lie

Four sons, the bearers
of the coffin
when I die

Bearhugs

Whenever my sons call round we hug each other.
Bearhugs. Both bigger than me and stronger
They lift me off my feet, crushing the life out of me.

They smell of oil paint and aftershave, of beer
Sometimes and tobacco, and of women
Whose memory they seem reluctant to wash away.

They haven't lived with me for years,
Since they were tiny, and so each visit
Is an assessment, a reassurance of love unspoken.

I look for some resemblance to my family.
Seize on an expression, a lifted eyebrow,
A tilt of the head, but cannot see myself.

Though like each other, they are not like me.
But I can see in them something of my father.
Uncles, home on leave during the war.

At three or four, I loved those straightbacked men
Towering above me, smiling and confident.
The whole world before them. Or so it seemed.

I look at my boys, slouched in armchairs
They have outgrown. See Tom in army uniform
And Finn in air force blue. Time is up.

Bearhugs. They lift me off my feet
And fifty years fall away. One son
After another, crushing the life into me.

Defying Gravity

Gravity is one of the oldest tricks in the book.
Let go of the book and it abseils to the ground
As if, at the centre of the earth, spins a giant yo-yo
To which everything is attached by an invisible string.

Tear out a page of the book and make an aeroplane.
Launch it. For an instant it seems that you have fashioned
A shape that can outwit air, that has slipped the knot.
But no. The earth turns, the winch tightens, it is wound in.

One of my closest friends is, at the time of writing,
Attempting to defy gravity, and will surely succeed.
Eighteen months ago he was playing rugby,
Now, seven stones lighter, his wife carries him aw-

Kwardly from room to room. Arranges him gently
Upon the sofa for the visitors. 'How are things?'
Asks one, not wanting to know. Pause. 'Not too bad.'
(Open brackets. Condition inoperable. Close brackets.)

Soon now, the man that I love (not the armful of bones)
Will defy gravity. Freeing himself from the tackle
He will sidestep the opposition and streak down the wing
Towards a dimension as yet unimagined.

Back where the strings are attached there will be a service
And homage paid to the giant yo-yo. A box of left-overs
Will be lowered into a space on loan from the clay.
Then, weighted down, the living will walk wearily away.

The Man in the Moon

On the edge of the jumping-off place I stood
Below me, the lake
Beyond that, the dark wood
And above, a night-sky that roared.

I picked a space between two stars
Held out my arms, and soared.

* * *

The journey lasted not half a minute
There is a moon reflected in the lake
You will find me in it.

6

The Elements

Oxygen

I am the very air
you breathe
Your first
and last
breath

I welcomed you
at birth
Shall bid
farewell
at death

I am the Kiss of Life
Its ebb and flow
With your last gasp
You will call my name:
'o o o o o o o o'

Nitrogen

'O' is for Oxygen
so gregarious
whereas I am
colourless
odourless
and tasteless
unattractive you might say
unreactive in every way
nitrogen: the night
to oxygen's day

I am 75 per cent
of the air you breathe
so keep me clean
For when I latch on
to fumes that cars exhaust
I am poison
Nitro-glycerine
that's me as well   Dynamite
I can blow you all to hell

But I'm not without
a sense of humour
N_2O is the proof, nitrous oxide
Inhale some laughing gas
and see my funny side

N is my symbol
N for nebulous
necessary
and nondescript.

Carbon

I am an atom of carbon
And carbon is the key
I am the element of life
And you owe yours to me

I am the glue of the Universe
The fixative
used by the Great Model-maker
I play a waiting game
Lie low that's my secret
Take a breath every millennium

But though set in my ways
Don't be misled. I'm not inert
I will go down in cosmic history
as an adventurer
For when I do make a move
Things happen and fast

I am an atom of carbon
And carbon is the key
I am the element of life
And you owe yours to me

When the tune is called
I carry the message
to the piper
Take the lead
in the decorous dance
of life and death

Patient, single-minded and stable
I keep my talents hidden
Bide my time
Until by Time am bidden.

Iron

Fe fi fo fum
As hard as nails
As tough as they come

I'm the most important
Metal known to man
(though aluminium
is more common
do we need another can?)

Five per cent of the earth's crust
I am also the stone at its centre
Iron fist in iron glove
Adding weight to the system
I am the firma in the terra

Fe fi fo
Don't drop me on your toe

My hobbies are space travel
And changing the course of history
(they even named an Age after me
– eat your heart out Gold)

And changing shape of course
From axe heads and plough shares
To masks maidens and missiles
I am malleable

I bend to your will
I am both the sword and the shield
The bullet and the forceps

I am all around you
And more much more
You are all around me 2, 3, 4 . . .

You've got me
Under your skin
I'm in your blood
What a spin that I'm in
Haemoglobin
You've got me
Under your skin

So strike while I'm hot
For if I'm not there
What are you?
Anaemic that's what

Fe fi
High and mighty
Iron

Gregarious and fancy-free
Easy going that's me
No hidden depths
I'm not elusive
To be conclusive
You get what you see
Fe Fe

Mercury

I repose at great speed
The joker in the pack
I cannot be fathomed
and turn your preconceptions
upside-down

You'll find me attractive
But I'm bad
(a poisoned chalice)
Hatters did
and they went mad
(ask Alice)

Alchemists
throughout the years
have been besotted by me
And understandably

I promised Gold
immortality
The secret of eternal youth

What I delivered
was Death
A stab in the back
As befits
The joker in the pack

Quicksilver
I am a messenger
And the message that I bring
is . . .

Sulphur

I'm what gets witches
a bad name
Funny smells
Gobbledy spells
Given to theatrics
I go in for special effects:
Brimstone and treacle
Hellfire. Eureka!
Gold! The Elixir of Life! Immortality!

Chinese alchemists were obsessed
Emperors were impressed
But in Beijing
I couldn't stop them
– ageing
And so they died
(But not in vain)
For a potion more mundane
was chanced upon
The Chinese called it:
'Fire Drug'

Mobsters
got where they got with it . . .
Children
play a lot with it . . .
Cities
glow white hot with it . . .
Guy Fawkes
hatched a plot with it . . .

Gunpowder.

Gold

I'm not a colour
Let's get that one straight
right from the start
Sunsets   Daffodils   Eagles
All take my name in vain
For vanity it is
Let me explain:

I'm the heart of things   The core
The Emperor of metals
Hence, *or*
Without me, commerce
would grind to a halt.
No money   No trade
Civilization (as you wish to know it)
simply fade

Of course, I can bring out the worse
I admit
That people kill for me
That rivers of blood
have been shed in my name
But that's you   Not me.
I'm not to blame

I glister
Am all show   All style
My aim is simple
To make you smile

Come closer:
If you had gold
and were offered something else
Would you swap?
No
You see, I've every right to crow

Le Coq d'or
. . . The one on top

Fool's Gold

I'm not real gold
A sham
Pyrite is what I am

But I'm gold to the touch
And look like gold as well
So who can tell?

Except the scientist
(this alchemist who casts a spell
exposing me)
But I don't care
I had a good run for my money

Besides
All gold is fool's gold
For what is it after all?
Bright yellow dung?
The sun's tears?
Satan's urine?
Gold
All who love you are fools.

Element 109

A mayfly blinks
I have lived and died
a thousand times
Mine is a short life
but an exciting one
I am man-made
and owe my existence
to science
I have no name
merely a number:
109. It suits me

I could go on
for hours and hours
about my various properties
But I won't

Now you see me
Now you . . .

READ MORE IN PENGUIN

A SELECTION OF POETRY

American Verse
British Poetry Since 1945
Caribbean Verse in English
Contemporary American Poetry
Contemporary British Poetry
English Poetry 1918–60
English Romantic Verse
English Verse
First World War Poetry
German Verse
Greek Verse
Irish Verse
Japanese Verse
Love Poetry
The Metaphysical Poets
Modern African Poetry
New Poetry
Poetry of the Thirties
Scottish Verse
Spanish Verse
Women Poets

READ MORE IN PENGUIN

A SELECTION OF PLAYS

Edward Albee	**Who's Afraid of Virginia Woolf?**
Alan Ayckbourn	**Joking Apart and Other Plays**
Dermot Bolger	**A Dublin Quartet**
Bertolt Brecht	**Parables for the Theatre**
Anton Chekhov	**Plays (The Cherry Orchard/Three Sisters/ Ivanov//The Seagull/Uncle Vania)**
Henrik Ibsen	**A Doll's House/League of Youth/Lady from the Sea**
Eugène Ionesco	**Rhinoceros/The Chairs/The Lesson**
Ben Jonson	**Three Comedies (Volpone/The Alchemist/ Bartholomew Fair)**
D. H. Lawrence	**Three Plays (The Collier's Friday Night/ The Daughter-in-Law/The Widowing of Mrs Holroyd)**
Arthur Miller	**Death of a Salesman**
John Mortimer	**A Voyage Round My Father/What Shall We Tell Caroline?/The Dock Brief**
J. B. Priestley	**Time and the Conways/I Have Been Here Before/An Inspector/The Linden Tree**
Peter Shaffer	**Lettice and Lovage/Yonadab**
Bernard Shaw	**Plays Pleasant (Arms and the Man/ Candida /The Man of Destiny/You Never Can Tell)**
Sophocles	**Three Theban Plays (Oedipus the King/ Antigone/ Oedipus at Colonus)**
Wendy Wasserstein	**The Heidi Chronicles and Other Plays**
Keith Waterhouse	**Jeffrey Bernard is Unwell and Other Plays**
Arnold Wesker	**Plays, Volume 1: The Wesker Trilogy (Chicken Soup with Barley/Roots/I'm Talking about Jerusalem)**
Oscar Wilde	**The Importance of Being Earnest and Other Plays**
Thornton Wilder	**Our Town/The Skin of Our Teeth/The Matchmaker**
Tennessee Williams	**Cat on a Hot Tin Roof/The Milk Train Doesn't Stop Here Anymore/The Night of the Iguana**

READ MORE IN PENGUIN

A SELECTION OF FICTION AND NON-FICTION

A Start in Life Anita Brookner

Now forty, Dr Ruth Weiss looks back and tells the story of a life impassioned and seduced by literature. As she recalls her London childhood, her friendships and doomed Parisian love affairs, she knows that once again she must make a start in life.

The Shape of Love Gelsey Kirkland and Greg Lawrence

In this compelling sequel to her bestselling *Dancing on My Grave,* Gelsey Kirkland takes up the story as she returns to the London stage to star as Juliet in *Romeo and Juliet* and Princess Aurora in *Sleeping Beauty*. 'Heart-rending ... the very image of passion' – *Observer*

The Life and Death of Mary Wollstonecraft Claire Tomalin

'Wide, penetrating, sympathetic ... there is no better book on Mary Wollstonecraft, nor is there likely to be ... The author brings a deep understanding to a remarkably complex woman ... but it is more than a biography: it illuminates the radical world of the 1780s and 1790s as few others do' – *New Statesman*

Isabelle Annette Kobak
The Life of Isabelle Eberhardt

'A European turned Arab, a Christian turned Muslim, a woman dressed as a man; a libertine who stilled profound mystical cravings by drink, hashish and innumerable Arab lovers ... All the intricate threads of her rebellious life are to be found in Annette Kobak's scrupulously researched book' – *Daily Telegraph*

Going Too Far Caroline Lassalle

On the terrace of a Greek villa Bettina and her guests – malicious, unstable Johnny and dedicated but excessive Delia – pass the morning, afternoon and evening of one day in quarrels, reminiscences and the telling of classical myths and legends. 'A brilliant and emotionally satisfying book' – *Sunday Times*

READ MORE IN PENGUIN

A SELECTION OF FICTION AND NON-FICTION

Money for Nothing P. G. Wodehouse

Lester Carmody of Rudge Hall is not altogether a good egg. Rather the reverse, in fact. For his intention is to inherit a large sum from the family silver by arranging its theft... 'His whimsical, hilarious stories aimed to do nothing more than amuse' – *Sunday Express*

Lucky Jim Kingsley Amis

'Dixon makes little dents in the smug fabric of hypocritical, humbugging, classbound British society ... Amis caught the mood of post-war restiveness in a book which, though socially significant, was, and still is, extremely funny' – Anthony Burgess

The Day Gone By Richard Adams

'He is the best adventure-story-writer alive ... Answers to the literary and personal puzzles of the Mr Adams phenomenon lie buried like truffles in his admirable autobiography' – A. N. Wilson in the *Daily Telegraph*

Romancing Vietnam Justin Wintle

'Justin Wintle's journal is a memorable, often amusing, always interesting diary of a tour of duty in a land where sharp-end history pokes round every corner' – *Yorkshire Post*. 'Compelling reading' – *Sunday Telegraph*

Travelling the World Paul Theroux

Now, for the first time, Paul Theroux has authorized a book of his favourite travel writing, containing photographs taken by those who have followed in his footsteps. The exquisite pictures here brilliantly complement and illuminate the provocative, wry, witty commentaries of one of the world's greatest travellers.

READ MORE IN PENGUIN

A SELECTION OF FICTION AND NON-FICTION

Yours Etc. Graham Greene

'An entertaining celebration of Graham Greene's lesser-known career as a prolific author of letters to newspapers; you will find unarguable proof of his total addiction to everything about his time, from the greatest issues of the day to the humblest subjects imaginable' – Salman Rushdie in the *Observer*

Just Looking John Updike

'Mr Updike can be a very good art critic, and some of these essays are marvellous examples of critical explanation ... A deep understanding of the art emerges' – *The New York Times Book Review*

As I Walked Out One Midsummer Morning Laurie Lee

As I Walked Out One Midsummer Morning tells of a young man's search for adventure as he leaves his Cotswolds home for London and Spain. 'A beautiful piece of writing' – *Observer*

The Secret Lemonade Drinker Guy Bellamy

Before Bobby met and married Caroline he believed in sex, drink and a good time. He still does... 'Sparkling ... It cracks open a thousand jokes, some old, some new and some blue. As hideously addictive as drink' – *Sunday Times*

A Thief in the Night John Cornwell

A veil of suspicion and secrecy surrounds the final hours of John Paul I, who died of a reported heart attack in September 1978. Award-winning crime-writer John Cornwell was invited by the Vatican to conduct a full investigation and his extraordinary findings are revealed here.

For Good or Evil Clive Sinclair

'The stories are not only very finely poised but genuinely contemporary, stylistically serious... a striking collection' – *The Times Literary Supplement*

READ MORE IN PENGUIN

A SELECTION OF FICTION AND NON-FICTION

Brightside G. H. Morris

Stuffed with magic, coal grit and wayward, Rabelaisian humour, this wonderful trilogy chronicles the lives of three generations of the Brightsides – a family with an appetite for the extraordinary. 'We've just mined a seam of home-produced – and Northern – magic realism' – *Observer*

Chasing the Monsoon Alexander Frater

In 1987 Alexander Frater decided to pursue the astonishing phenomenon of the Indian summer monsoon and this fascinating account of his journey reveals the exotic, often startling discoveries of an ambitious and irresistibly romantic adventure.

Love in the Time of Cholera Gabriel García Márquez

'For fifty years a breath-taking beauty, now old and just widowed, has recoiled in pride and guilt from her secret lover. His desolate obsession has led him into an enigmatic existence in spite of his renown in business. One Pentecost, love found a new tongue with which to speak. Unique Márquez magic of the sadness and funniness of humanity' – *The Times*

The Invisible Woman Claire Tomalin

'Made visible is Nelly Ternan, and in the process, Tomalin gives us the world of a nineteenth-century actress and most importantly, the real world of Charles Dickens, whose passion for her ... changed his life, his career and his work' – Melvyn Bragg in the *Independent*

Shots from the Hip Charles Shaar Murray

His classic encapsulation of the moment when rock stars turned junkies as the sixties died; his dissection of rock 'n' roll violence as citizens assaulted the Sex Pistols; his superstar encounters, from the decline of Paul McCartney to Mick Jagger's request that the author should leave – Charles Shaar Murray's *Shots from the Hip* is also rock history in the making.

BY THE SAME AUTHOR

Blazing Fruit
Selected Poems 1967–1987

'A poet for us all: laconic, ironic, at times Byronic – he swims the Hellespont and bridges the Watford Gap' – Laurie Lee

'McGough has developed a fine ear for timing, and a number of his poems turn superbly on the rhetoric of surprise . . . His humour tends to be of the dark kind, reflecting that cynicism which, coupled with his ingenious exploitation of puns, has become his trademark' – David Profumo in the *Literary Review*

'Witty, satirical, sketch-like poems on society which also hit hard at a few home truths . . . McGough is what poets should be . . . a people's poet' – Martin Booth in *British Book News*

Summer with Monika

Summer with Monika charts the bittersweet fall of a love affair from joy through jealousy to the time when love becomes 'as nice as a cup of tea in bed'. Peter Blake's illustrations perfectly complement what is now a classic of Sixties popular culture, McGough's most tender, wry and witty 'once upon a love' story.

'Sharp and sparkling, his words have a way of wrapping themselves round the hearts of people . . . Certainly no disillusioned lover in the land can read *Summer with Monika* without getting a lump in the throat' – Val Hennessy in *Time Out*

'A considerable voice, quirky, compassionate . . . his ability to make us smile and be sad at the same time is McGough's great gift' – Neil Philip

also published:

Melting into the Foreground